MW00915575

False Prophets

*Do We Keep Smiling
and Say Nothing?*

Ernie Gruen

False Prophets

Do We Keep Smiling and Say Nothing?

Copyright © 1990 by Ernie Gruen

All rights reserved

ISBN 9781726786232

Printed in the United States of America

Unless otherwise stated, all Scripture quotations are taken from The New American Standard Bible (NASB) © The Lockman Foundation, 1960, 1962, 1968, 1971, 1973, 1975, 1977.

Contents

Do We Keep Smiling and Say Nothing? 1

Letter 27

Interview 37

Testimony 41

Index 47

Do We Keep Smiling and Say Nothing?

I N MATTHEW 24 we have the passage about the last days. I want to bring to your attention three sections, starting with verses 4 and 5:

> Jesus answered and said to them, "See to it that no one misleads you. For *many* will come in My name saying 'I am the Christ' and will *mislead many.*" (NASB)

And then Jesus returns to that theme in verse 11:

> "*Many* false prophets will arise and will *mislead many.* Because lawlessness is increased, most people's love will grow cold. But the one who endures to the end, he will be saved."

Jesus returns to that theme again in verse 23:

"Then if anyone says to you, 'Behold, here is the Christ,' or 'There He is,' do not believe him. For false Christs and false prophets will arise and will show great signs and wonders, so as to mislead, if possible, even the elect. Behold, I have told you in advance. So if they say to you, 'Behold, He is in the wilderness,' do not go out, or, 'Behold, He is in the inner rooms,' do not believe them."

Colossians 2:8:

See to it that no one takes you captive through philosophy and empty deception, according to the tradition of men, according to the elementary principles of the world, rather than according to Christ. For in Him all the fullness of Deity dwells in bodily form, and in Him you have been made complete.

Colossians 2:18:

Let no one keep defrauding you of your prize by delighting in self-abasement and the worship of the angels, taking his stand on visions he has seen, inflated without cause by his fleshly mind, and not holding fast to the head, from whom the entire body, being supplied and held together by the joints and ligaments, grows with a growth which is from God.

If you have died with Christ to the elementary principles of the world, why, as if you were living in the world, do you submit yourself to decrees, such as, "Do not handle, do not taste, do not touch!" (which all refer to things destined to perish with use)—in accordance with the commandments and teachings of men? These are matters which have, to be sure, the appearance of wisdom in self-made religion and self-abasement and severe treatment of the body, but are of no value against fleshly indulgence.

Today I want to talk about a problem in our city. A key family in this church asked me a question this week. It is a question I have asked myself for at least five years. The question is: *Do we keep smiling and say nothing?*

You know there is a time to say something, and this morning I'm instructed by the Lord to say something. I've said a few things before. In the summer of '86 I preached a message on how you distinguish the characteristics of a cult and a church. And, then, about two years ago, I preached an entire message on the fact *Kansas City is filled with false prophets.*

The thing that pushes my button today perhaps is the Jeffrey Lundgren story. In our city, in our own metroplex, a man began to say he was a prophet. He ruined and destroyed many families after he misled them. They began to worship him and worship his prophecies. He murdered five people. In the latest report I think I heard 13 people of that cult group have been arrested for murder or accessory thereof. This is the danger of following a man or a prophet or someone who is a self-proclaimed prophet.

You know there are a lot of people who want some-one to tell them what to do. I want to issue a clear warning, because Jesus, while He mentions wars and rumors of wars, earthquakes—and we get all excited about that—just a casual reading of Matthew 24 says the two things that mark the last days are *false prophets* and *deception.*

He says take care that no one misleads you. He says there will be many false prophets. Then He talks about wars and rumors of wars, earthquakes, comes back again, repeats Himself, intensifies it—He even says *many* false prophets will deceive *many.* He says there is going to be a whole bunch of them and they are going to be highly successful. Very sad, but it has to come true, because the Lord prophesied it. He said many false prophets will deceive many. The love of many will wax cold.

Then Jesus goes on to something else, talks about a time of tribulation such as the world has not faced, which probably refers to a nuclear holocaust, whether we like it or not. But that isn't really the simple point of

Matthew 24. He takes another run at it! And the third time He says: *Don't believe them! I have told you in advance!* Three times here in Matthew 24 Jesus mentions false prophets.

I want you to know I searched my heart about this message and prayed about every sentence of it. There's no jealousy in my heart. There are no evil or bad motives. But I am forced to speak today as a father in this city. The Bible says to think soberly. I don't think I'm a big deal, but I do think, in some sense, I am one of the fathers of Kansas City.

About four years ago, I had a dream, and in the dream I stood up here and preached this message. In the dream I said, "I don't want to preach this message. But I have to preach it." I sat on it for four years. I prayed about it almost weekly for four years, trying to make sure I wasn't unduly influenced by a dream. I wanted to be convinced it was from the Lord.

Last night, as I woke out of my sleep in the middle of the night, I saw a huge black spider on the wall of Kansas City. I was up here last night praying. The Lord won't let me do anything but obey Him.

At one point when we lived in the country, my wife happened to be in Israel and my daughter Cheryl was with me because she wasn't married yet. I heard a huge scream. It sounded like somebody being attacked!

I ran towards her to find out what had happened. She was coming out of the hallway bathroom having just seen a huge spider. It was at least five inches across. I'm counting legs. It was in the stool.

"No problem," I said with great bravery to my daughter.

I flushed the toilet, but that spider was so big it held on. That thing could not be flushed down—that is how big it was.

I went and got the plumber's friend, flushed it again, and, with a lot of suction from the plumber's friend, the spider finally went down.

That's what I saw on the wall of this city.

So I'm forced today by the Holy Ghost to be obedient and to be a father and to speak as one of the fathers over the city.

I want to read a couple other Scriptures. I Timothy 1:20: "Among these are Hymenaeus and Alexander, whom I have handed over to Satan." II Timothy 3:8: "Just as Jannes and Jambres opposed Moses, so these men also oppose the truth, men of depraved mind, rejected in regard to the faith."

Those verses give you the Scriptural basis for naming names. The apostles named names and I will have to name some names, too; however, I'm going to be very careful, and very discreet, and very, very kind.

First of all, in Colossians—I'm back in Colossians 2—Paul rebukes this wonderful church. It evidently was given to mysticism. In one of the most beautiful chapters in the Bible he says we're complete in Jesus

Christ. But the context of that tenth verse is that eighth verse: "Don't let anyone take you captive to philosophy and empty deception." This church had been taken captive! We don't know the details, but the apostle Paul says here in verse 18: "Let no one keep defrauding you of your prize."

The word "defraud" means "to deprive of some possession by deceit." Somehow this church (or this city) was being cheated! Someone was defrauding them of their prize—of their possession!

I believe one of the most wonderful possessions that we have is stability, rest and peace. Do you agree with that? That's what this church has stood for: doctrine of stability and rest and peace. But now what we have in the city is chaos and confusion and charismatic excess. Three c's: charismatic excess, chaos and confusion. People are being defrauded and hurt.

Unfortunately when something happens in the city, it isn't just a matter of whether it's nice or not; people get hurt. I'm thinking of Agape Ministries when that church closed. Some of those people are in our church now. A lot of those people are my friends. But there are literally hundreds and thousands of people who no longer go to church because they got into a movement that was not of God, not born of God, and now they are shipwrecked and ruined.

Paul rebukes the church at Colossae. Don't let anyone defraud you of your prize. The second phrase he says is "delighting in self-abasement." That's an interesting phrase. Verses 20, 21, and 22 kind of expand that: "If you have died with Christ to the elementary principles of the world, why, as if you were living in the world, do you submit yourself to decrees?" Some preacher with a bunch of rules: don't touch, don't handle, don't taste. He said all those rules perish because of the commandments and teachings of men. See that in verse 22?

In our city now we have a new monasticism. Teachings about money. Legalisms and rules. Delighting in being monastic—withdrawing from society, or to use the Scriptural phrase, self-abasement.

He is rebuking them: don't let them defraud you, steal from you, take away your possession in Christ, and don't let them delight in self-abasement.

Then he mentions the worship of angels. Let no one keep defrauding you of your prize by delighting in self-abasement and worship of angels. The Greek word "angel" means "messenger." For example, the letters to the seven churches, to the "angel" of the church of Ephesus, the "angel" of the church of Smyrna, the "angel" of the church of Laodicea.

Some people say that's the pastor, so it should be translated not angel in the sense of supernatural being, but I'm not sure in this passage whether it means human messengers or angels. However, let's just take it both ways. Paul really rebuked this church. You are worshipping angels, he said. You are worshipping messengers.

FALSE PROPHETS

Now we have a prophet in town who says angels speak to him. We've got a horrible problem in this city. I guess the question is: do we just keep smiling and say nothing? Well, today I have to say something because I'm instructed by the Lord to do it.

We had a prophet in this city who prophesied over a mother with a baby that it was to be born at home. I am talking about Kansas City Fellowship. Now I'm not going to name many human names. I am going to tell you whom I am talking about.

Midterm the mother begins to feel nervous about not going to an OB doctor. So she goes to the doctor.

"Hey, something here isn't right," the doctor says.

"That's unbelief! You go by our prophecy!" the prophets said.

She had the baby—at home—and it died.

That's the kind of thing that forces me to say something, because these kinds of prophecies are never announced or mentioned or hyped.

Then you had a prophecy: "There is going to be a terrible winter snow storm that will cut off all electricity in the first week or two of January." Obviously it was a lie—it never happened—it was false prophecy. The prophecy said the grocery stores would be empty. "There will be no electricity. It will be weeks before they can get the power back on."

The thing is people don't know that this "prophet" had prophesied a winter storm regularly in this city for years—and he had been rejected! Now that is a false prophecy!

These tapes circulate in our home groups, and I have people come to me and ask, "Shall we just keep smiling and say nothing?"

We had the prophecy of a 1988 stock market crash. There was one in '87, you remember, so the prophet said it would happen again in October. It didn't. People pulled money out of the stock market—I could care less about that. My point is there is no accountability! There is no responsibility! It's people worshipping angels, worshipping messengers.

Then we had a big prophecy saying three years after Kansas City Fellowship began there would be a revival so great thousands and hundreds of thousands of people would be saved in Kansas City. It was trumpeted and proclaimed and people got excited and they got a crowd. But it didn't happen. It was a false prophecy.

Now they have a new prophecy. "The National Football League, Major League Baseball, and the National Basketball Association—they're all going to close down." They won't. They are false prophecies—and it's weird.

One of these prophets has been from church to church and his ministry was repudiated by pastor after pastor. He said in one church everybody should go home and sprinkle baking powder on their bathroom stool and then flush it down as a sign of purity of the house.

"What's your opinion of the prophecy?" someone asked me.

"We'd have flushed it here!" I quipped.

Can you imagine our elders putting up with a prophecy like that for two minutes?

This same prophet supposedly once knew about adultery in a youth group.

"Seven people will drop dead!" he prophesied.

(Because this is in print maybe some of you have read it; I've got it in my briefcase.)

I have checked with the pastor. The truth is one person died in that church who was nearly 100 years old. Another person died who was in the Navy; but he hadn't been to church in a couple years. Two other people died in a motorcycle wreck. The article says all seven people who died were under 30. But none of those four people were under 30. It was a total, outright fabrication. It just isn't true.

"What do you think of Bob Jones?" I asked Mike Bickle.

"Only 60 percent of his prophecies come true," Bickle said, "And he's a problem to me. I had to sit him down. I don't let him prophesy."

Yet you pick up *Charisma* magazine and it says he's a noble prophet recognized all over Kansas City. Why is it privately he's called a problem and most of his prophecies don't come true, and yet publicly for hype's sake he's portrayed to the nation as exceptional? Well, it's not for me to judge the motives; but those are the facts. So we've got a problem.

Look at the next phrase in the Scripture: "taking his stand on visions he's seen." Let me remind you that's not stated here in a positive sense. "Taking his stand on visions he's seen." This is a rebuke. You have to watch out, I believe.

We are getting all kinds of phone calls from pastors about how in their Christian school their kids are getting "caught up to the third heaven"; and they are "praying to see angels"; or "seeing angels"; or are "seeing prophecies."

From my perspective this is a dangerous manipulation of children. If you were to go out to our children's church, for example, you could get their attention.

"Now kids, there's a hell. It's full of fire, and anyone who gets sent to hell will burn there forever. There's one way to not go to hell and that's to accept Jesus. How many of you kids would like to accept Jesus this morning in children's church?"

How many conversions are you going to get? You're going to get a lot of hands. How many of you know that would be an improper way of handling children? I would not permit it and we will not permit our school administrators or teachers to pull that kind of number on innocent little elementary-age kids.

They went and bought a new piece of property. The elders decided they would take a couple kids and walk them through the property, and let the school children tell the elders what demons were going up and down; so they can bind the demons and cleanse the property.

You may think that's wonderful. I think it's terrible. You hear these kinds of things and some people get all excited and upset.

"Why aren't the children at Maranatha seeing angels?!"

Because we're not into praying to angels or worshipping angels!

Paul continues to rebuke them. You delighted in self-abasement, worship of angels, taking a stand on visions. The fifth phrase is "inflated without cause by his fleshly mind."

Today I'm basically going to tell you everything I know about this aberration in our city. I believe the whole city and the whole nation is being harmed.

We went through ten stages with Kansas City Fellowship (KCF). The first stage was a Receiving stage. When Mike Bickle first arrived in town, I welcomed him with open arms. I let him speak to our Charismatic Pastors Fellowship. I put him on a steering committee along with me and another brother to plan the Charismatic Fellowship.

"He's off!" a brother warned me sternly. "He's strange—and you're going to get burned—badly!"

"Has he started doing it yet, what he did to St. Louis?" a pastor asked me.

"Doing what?" I asked.

"Steal members. His method of operation is to destroy other churches by stealing members."

I ignored all the warnings and received him completely.

The second stage we had was what I call the Supposed Submission stage. He used my name. There was never a formal nor informal agreement on my part (or even a suggestion) that he should submit to me. Yet down there he constantly said otherwise.

"Ernie Gruen is my best friend," Mike Bickle said. "I call Ernie all the time. I submit to him."

This was all a fabrication.

We once had a Charismatic Pastors Fellowship with all the city pastors. Still in the Receiving stage, I let him teach. In the middle of his message, he began to teach that apostles could not be married and could not own property; and that prophets could be married, but couldn't own property. In other words, prophets could not own property, but could be married; whereas apostles, neither one.

"That's Roman Catholicism," I stated, interrupting his class. "That's false teaching. That's *heresy!*"

"Well, I didn't say that," he later said, instead of recanting.

But one of his own staff corrected him at a meeting.

"Mike," he objected, "you *did* say it—and you didn't say it hypothetically."

So he wasn't in submission at all. The first time we disagreed on what I considered a major point of heresy there was the absence of submission.

Then there was the Government by Prophets stage. This was where the whole church was run by prophets. There were no elders initially.

Now I am going to be blunt. I was sure one of the supposed prophets who was running the church was a homosexual. I hoped it wasn't true, but I thought at least he was effeminate.

So I got on the phone, called St. Louis, called Phoenix, called some pastors I knew.

"Yeah," they said, "we all know the man is a homosexual."

"What's your evidence?" I asked.

"We don't have any."

It was just rumor, slander, or gossip, so I ignored it. There was nothing I could do until a friend of mine, who is a pastor, told me the story of how this prophet behaved when he, the pastor, was a young Christian.

While they were driving down the highway, the prophet reached over and started playing with his knees. The pastor thought it was a little strange; he pulled away.

After they got to the motel room it got worse.

"I want to do what Elisha did," the prophet said. "I want you to take off all your clothes and lay naked, and I'm going to lay naked on top of you and breathe with my mouth the breath of life into your body."

Totally alarmed, my friend, the pastor, ran from the motel room. He was then a relatively new Christian.

They have never repudiated that man's prophecies! He has prophesied over pastors all over this city! Even this year they have announced with great excitement that this man's prophecies helped the church be founded "prophetically."

So what do you do? Keep smiling and say nothing? That's what my church people ask me. "What do we say?!" That was the Government by Prophets stage.

Then we have the Usurpation stage. This was where they begin to take over churches. When Larry Lea was in town down at one church, and while he was holding a meeting, they gathered and had a private meeting in the Sunday School room. They prophesied for people to leave a church that was connected to us, and become a part of Kansas City Fellowship.

Well, that drove me crazy!

I told John Arnold.

"You knew it would happen to you, didn't you?" he said.

"What do you mean?" I asked.

"Well," he explained, "when a minister was up here from Florida, and he was speaking with all the pastors in a children's church, they gathered a bunch of prophets at the Sunday school room here and had their own meeting."

So usurpation begins. People were coming to this prayer meeting and eventually became part of his staff.

Next we went to the Matthew 18 stage. I went to lunch with him, confronted him, but it accomplished nothing. Basically there was no problem. All smiles. Very fake.

So I jumped a step. Get two or three brothers. I got Howard and Art along with Don from East and Jim from South. Jeff and some other elders were there. We probably had 15 people. There were about six people from KCF.

In alluding to one incident where I had sat him down, their leader challenged me.

"You touched me illegally," Mike Bickle said to my face. "People who touched me illegally—bad things happen to them—things like death. Other people who touched me illegally have died."

It was a terrible meeting. I could not imagine a worse meeting. I was so upset that I could not even discuss it with my wife for three days. I was upset spiritually and emotionally. I finally told my wife what he had said, and how I felt like I had been threatened with death.

"You're kidding!" she exclaimed. "He walked out of that room, walked down the hall, was all smiles, and said, 'Your husband is one of the neatest men of

God I have ever met!' That's why I didn't ask you any questions; I assumed you were best friends!"

We had a third meeting with all the elders. This meeting was just basically all flowers. "I'm sorry I said that." "Anything you brought up—you're right!" Smiles. It was totally superficial.

So we did do a Matthew 18—and I guess this is bringing it before the whole church—and the church will have to decide.

I skipped the Monastic Mysticism stage which basically describes their ministry.

Then we went to the Aggressive Prophetic Expansion stage. This is where they begin to prophesy that churches should close and be part of their ministry. They did it three times I can document, but actually more than that. Sermons were preached on "How You Know When to Close a Church." And then they had a prophet along that said: "You are to close your church down. All become part of KCF."

I'm getting more and more frustrated—*How long do I smile and say nothing when the city is being torn apart!? What's my responsibility to the city? I'll preach this message. I'll be the dirty dog. Everyone will look down their nose at me and question my motives, but I could care less, because I'm obeying God.*

Somebody has to say something! And it needs to come from a senior pastor. We need to know everything—and I know this tape will go all over—but it needs to—it needs to go from the west coast to the east coast.

A few months ago, John Arnold and I met with an Assembly of God pastor who wanted to become a network church.

"It would be unethical for you to become a network church," I cautioned, "when you are in the Assembly of God denomination."

His district overseer was Bill Newby, who attends our Charismatic Pastors Fellowship. He is a wonderful man and personal friend. I love Bill Newby of Central Assembly.

"If you leave the Assembly of God," I advised this pastor, "you've got to sit down with Bill Newby and ask him how far away he will ask you to go to start a new church. That isn't the easy way, but it's the right way. That's taking up your cross, because you can't tear up that Assembly of God church."

"I wouldn't consider you being a network church," I added, "until you're out of the city for six months, until Bill Newby and you and I all sit in the same room, and I could know that Bill Newby hasn't been shafted."

He walked out of the room and spoke to Pastor Don.

"Well," he said, "I like Ernie Gruen and everything, but I don't agree with everything the man says."

Eight days later to the day, Mike Bickle went out, preached to the church and declared they should shut it down. He took a prophet, prophesied that the church should shut, took all the people, and put them in KCF. *Eight days later* (!) without even a thought of it being unethical.

I called Bill Newby.

"The word's out on you, Ernie," he said. "The Assembly of God pastors say, 'Ernie Gruen will never hurt one of our churches. One thing about Ernie is you can trust him. He's never done us dirty.'"

See, they are going, grabbing people, expanding. We won't—I don't want another church! I don't want to get bigger.

"Anyone can have integrity," Bill Newby said, "when it doesn't cost them anything." I thought that was one of the best sentences I'd heard in 1989. We are going to have integrity!

"KCF and a couple of their prophets are going to come out," a couple of our network guys told me. "They have seen a vision of three lights coming together and three lights being one light. They're going to come out and prophesy at three of our network churches."

"No, they aren't!" I said.

I offended those pastors and I hurt their feelings. I'm not saying I handled it perfectly, but I knew what was going to happen: they were going to get a prophecy.

"We don't go by personal prophecies!" everyone says. "We go by the Bible!" But I have seen three whole churches close after one prophecy. So, frankly, I don't believe people just go by the Bible. I just don't believe it. I believe the average Charismatic is a sitting duck and gullible. That was the Aggressive Prophetic Expansion stage by which I mean they take over churches by prophecy.

Stage 8: The Exaltation of Man. I was taken down there to a 90-minute meeting. The Bible was not opened. The Scripture was not read. Jesus was not mentioned. For 90 minutes all they talked about was this great prophet.

If I did that here at Full Faith my elders would have been after my case! Can you imagine preaching about a man, no matter how noble, for 90 minutes? Just to hype and PR? That was the Exaltation of Man stage.

Then we had the Absorption stage by which I mean they are absorbing churches. Can I just say it? Kansas City Fellowship doctrine is this: *All money comes to Grandview. All decisions are made by one elder board out of Grandview. "We'll take your people and your money and we'll be your elders."*

I don't believe that's Scriptural.

"What's the difference between them and us?" you ask.

North has their own elder board. East has their own elder board. All of our churches decide how they're going to spend their money. They keep their own money. I wrote every church should set its own vision, control its own money and make its own decisions. I do not believe in a supervised government where one church has absolute control. Their definition of unity is: *the big fish eats the little fish and they cease to exist.*

21

So all of a sudden now there is one group of elders for all the churches and it is making all the money decisions for the entire city. I believe that's dangerous and unscriptural. I know it's being hyped nationwide as "The New Testament Church." What they are starting to preach now is: "What we need is one church in the city."

They tried it in China; it didn't work there. It won't work here, either. How foolish for a few Charismatics to get together and say, "We're the Church in Kansas City." What about the Baptists and the Lutherans? What about the Assembly of God? But that's what's being told. You can guess whose church the one church will be.

Now, in case you hadn't caught on, we at Full Faith are not, have not, and will never be a part of KCF (Kansas City Fellowship). Why do I say that? I don't believe in what they are doing. I don't believe in their theology. I don't believe in their ethics. I don't believe in their prophecies.

And when that thing goes *really* weird, I don't want to be anywhere near, and I don't want anyone to say: "Well, we were submitted to Ernie Gruen." You never were submitted here. They've never had a thing to do with us. We've never had a thing to do with them. I'm not going to promote them or back them.

When that thing blows sky high, when thousands and thousands of people are hurt and wounded, this franchise disillusioned, I want it clear that they are not a part of Full Faith—have never been a part of Full Faith—*and never will be!*

My conclusion is they are opportunistic and unethical. They have an agenda to take over the city and the nation. They use Pied Piper–like prophecy and their church is off. There are people there who do have integrity, but they are still deceived. So I am not calling into question the integrity of everyone there—of course not.

Now the last verse in Colossians 2:23—look at this:

These are matters which have to be sure the appearance of wisdom and self-made religion and self-abasement and severe treatment of the body, but are of no value against fleshly indulgence.

Now that's verbatim Colossians 2:23. They won't help anyone get out of the flesh. I cannot tell you how much I prayed over this message—over every sentence—trying not to use any rhetoric—trying not in any way to overstate.

Jeremiah 17:5:

Thus says the Lord: *"Cursed is the man who trusts in man!* And makes flesh his strength. And whose heart turns away from the Lord. For he will be like a shrub in the desert and will not see when

23

prosperity comes. But will live in stony waste and will live in the wilderness, a land with salt and without inhabitant."

Now if you trust Ernie Gruen, I guarantee you've got a curse on you. You know why I really think Jim Bakker and Jimmy Swaggart fell? I think it's because a bunch of people started worshipping them. I wonder whether it's a judgment on them or a judgment on the Church. *There is no man noble enough to worship.* I guarantee you *if you put your faith in a prophet, you are cursed of God!*

You have a perfect right to disagree with this sermon. That's why I have always taught you to read the Bible through every year. And taught you to have a Quiet Time. And taught you to have a relationship with God. And taught you to have communion with God. And tried my very best to make sure you didn't look to me.

I want you to read the Bible for yourself—from cover to cover—so you would have a Biblical basis to examine every word I said. And you'd have the courage to say, "I love Ernie Gruen and everything, but that paragraph is wrong, because it says this and that in the Scripture." *Cursed is the man who trusts in man!*

I believe there is a place for prophecy. But I want to tell you something: I don't need a prophecy! Because I know what God is saying. Because I am with Him every day and I walk with Him. I don't need a prophecy to tell me what to do. That means I'm qualified to receive one, because I'm not looking for one. Does that make sense?

You know who is qualified to get married, you singles? It's the person who doesn't need a husband or wife. If you don't need to get married, you're qualified to get married. If you need to get married to be fulfilled, you will marry anything. There are some things worse than being single: marrying the wrong person.

The person who doesn't need to get married, who is fulfilled in Jesus, who walks with Jesus, whose emotional needs and everything are met in Christ Jesus, *that* person is ready to get married.

The person who doesn't need a prophecy is the person who is ready to receive one. If you are longing for a prophecy, you may get a bad one.

I am telling you this verse scares me if you take it seriously, if it really is true, particularly when you read the context of verse 9: *"the heart is deceitful, desperately wicked"*—*"deceitful above all things, desperately wicked—who can know it?"*

God says you're going to be like a little desert bush, sir, sister, if you looked to a man, because man's heart is desperately wicked and deceitful above all things. See that ninth verse tells you why you can't trust man.

So I have obeyed God. I'm at perfect peace with what I've said today. It needed to be said. What they do is out of my realm. They've got a circle. I've got a circle. But the circles do not overlap. Whatever they do is their business; it's between them and God. But I'm a little sick of them proselytizing the whole city through prophecy.

You want to go there, go, but don't go to both churches. They're of a different spirit and a different stream.

I pray for them. I sincerely hope that they get balanced out, and that they become a blessing and that thousands of people aren't hurt and destroyed.

You have now heard the answer to your question to me and my question to myself, "Do we keep smiling or say something?"

You feel free to say anything I said. Get a tape. Get anything you want. I'll see to it that the leaders at KCF get a copy of this tape.

"I really hate to preach this message," I told my wife, "because I'll tear up the city."

"Ernie," she said, "it is *they* who are tearing up the city. It is not Full Faith. It's not from you telling the truth."

I prayed for years since I had the dream to do this, and now I've done it. Now I feel like it's God's timing.

Letter

THIS OPEN LETTER summarizes our concerns about Mike Bickle and Kansas City Fellowship. I have known Mike Bickle since his arrival in Kansas City a little over seven years ago. We at Full Faith Church of Love are also well acquainted with many wonderful Christian brothers and sisters who attend there.

While there have often been controversies, strange stories, and troubling rumors associated with Kansas City Fellowship, I never sought to substantiate them; rather, I accepted Mike Bickle with open arms as a man of integrity who was trying to do something for the Lord. In fact, I even put him on the steering committee of the citywide Charismatic Pastors Fellowship, which is hosted by our church.

When people came to us who were upset with Mike, his methods of operation, and the prophecies, our attitude was, "Who in the ministry doesn't make mistakes?" Mike had our support and best wishes. It was hoped that these were simply growing pains which would take care of themselves in time.

However, in the last few years the situation really became serious, as it included accounts of wounded people, unethical practices, false prophecies, and damaged churches. Families reported how their lives had been tragically affected by their association with Kansas City Fellowship. The conviction grew in my spirit that something was very wrong. Finally, the Lord Jesus Christ laid it firmly on my heart that something had to be done.

I decided to obey Matthew 18. I met with Mike privately, and then met twice with Mike and members of his leadership group. These efforts proved fruitless. During the meetings, aspects of Mike's character which were extremely troubling came out. Mike Bickle delivered ominous spiritual warnings threatening me with harm. Our concerns were deepened rather than alleviated. Outer "lip service" reassurances by Mike never generated any real change of heart or practice.

On Saturday, January 20, while praying at the church, God told that if I didn't preach the message "Do We Keep Smiling and Say Nothing?" I would be disobedient to Him. I had no choice but speak out publicly to warn the Body of Christ. It wasn't something I wanted to do, but God was directing me to take a stand for the sake of His people.

As I was praying with my wife Dee on the Monday morning after I preached that sermon, she referred to a Scripture in Acts 18 which God had given us years ago when we first received the baptism of the Holy Spirit. The Lord impressed me to look it up and read it. The Scripture reads as follows:

"Do not be afraid any longer, but go on speaking and do not be silent; for I am with you, and no man will attack you in order to harm you, for I have many people in this city" (Acts 18:9-10).

I had been afraid because Mike Bickle implied my death if I took a stand against his teaching. But now the Lord was clearly speaking to me that I ought not be silent; that He would be with me; that no harm would come to me; and that I had to keep speaking because of the people in this city.

Mike has sought to portray our concerns as a "personality conflict," a problem of "misunderstanding and lack of communication," and even insecurity or jealousy on my part.

I want to assure you that I did not place 34 years of fruitful ministry and my national credibility on the line for any of these trivial reasons. The deep conviction of my heart is that we have, in Kansas City, the beginnings of a Charismatic heresy which is far more significant than the shepherding controversy. I believe that this could split the Body of Christ and cause untold damage to tens of thousands of Christians, as well as hundreds of churches across America.

Because all of this is happening in my back yard, and because we've witnessed firsthand the devastation that Mike's movement has wrought in area churches and lives, I have had no other choice but to speak, even though it is a task that I do not cherish. It is an assignment from the Lord that I would not wish on anyone.

The Lord spoke to me, "You are my point guard. You must take the ball and bring it up the court." He warned me, "Do not foul; do not step out of bounds." He also said: "You must know when to pass the ball to the taller players."

In this documentation we are attempting to be absolutely fair and accurate.

I want to humble myself by admitting three mistakes in my taped message "Do We Keep Smiling and Say Nothing?" All of the events described in the tape did actually happen, but some of the details weren't accurate. They are corrected as follows:

1. The story regarding prophecies that a woman should have her baby at home and the baby dying did happen; however, the prophecies occurred in a Kansas City Fellowship home group and were not given by a member of their staff. Again, the event was truth, but this detail was incorrect.

2. We have been able to document two churches that were taken over by Kansas City Fellowship in which

prophecy played a definite part. Ironically, the churches we have documented are two different churches from the ones indicated on the tape. The fact that they have used prophecy to close and/or take over churches is accurate; however these details are somewhat different.

3. The fabricated story that seven young people from Berean Baptist Church died—all in a six-week time frame—is a complete lie. However, the details surrounding these deaths and the people involved are much more complex than those which were reported on my tape. Included in our documentation is a clear summary of these events. Again, the substance of what I said was absolutely true, but a few of the minute details were not correct.

I want to apologize to Kansas City Fellowship, not for giving fabrications or gross distortions—I did not tell any lies or grossly distort anything—but for the errors in some of the details contained on the tape.

KCF's response has been to try to dismiss all of our concerns as unsubstantiated and based on rumor or misunderstanding because of the inaccuracy of the above details. The facts are, however, that the situation in KCF is much worse and far more serious than that which was depicted on my original tape.

Because of their intent to discredit the information on the tape, we found it necessary to carefully research the teachings, practices, and beliefs of KCF directly from their own messages. We've studied transcripts of KCF's tapes available to the general public, and have also used written, signed, personal testimonies given to us by the individuals and churches who have been harmed.

From these we have created a carefully documented analysis of KCF's beliefs, practices, and some of their mystical experiences. It has six sections and is over 200 pages long. We assure our readers that none of the quotes have been taken out of context. They are absolutely accurate and carefully reflect the intentions and meaning of the speaker when given. We have the original tapes which can be obtained from us if someone wishes to check our integrity or accuracy.

Before proceeding further, I wish to share some Scriptures. I have written this documentation with the fear of God and after a long personal fast. I was made for His glory; I certainly was not made to slander other Christians. Scriptures that give me the fear of God are Luke 6:37-38:

> And do not judge and you will not be judged; and do not condemn, and you will not be condemned; pardon, and you will be pardoned. Give, and it will be given to you; good measure, pressed down, shaken together, running over, they will pour into your lap. For by your standard of measure it will be measured to you in return.

In my heart I am certainly not trying to judge, condemn, or even criticize; rather I am trying to accurately report what I consider to be a budding Charismatic heresy. I also want to confess that I fear greatly sowing discord; in Proverbs 6:19 God says He hates it. (It is actually KCF who has sowed discord in our city.) If these were the only verses in the Bible, I would not furnish this documentation. However, there are other Scriptures in the Bible. Let me list a few:

1. "He who rebukes a man will afterward find more favor than he who flatters with the tongue" (Proverbs 28:23).

2. "For there will no longer be any false vision or flattering divination within the house of Israel" (Ezekiel 12:24).

3. "Do not be carried away by varied and strange teachings" (Hebrews 13:9a).

4. "For the time will come when they will not endure sound doctrine; but wanting to have their ears tickled, they will accumulate for themselves teachers in accordance to their own desires; and will turn away their ears from the truth, and will turn aside to myths" (II Timothy 4:34).

5. "A truthful witness saves lives, but he who speaks lies is treacherous" (Proverbs 14:25).

6. "As a result, we are no longer to be children, tossed here and there by waves, and carried about by every wind of doctrine, by the trickery of men, by craftiness, in deceitful scheming" (Ephesians 4:14).

This Scripture warns against seeking after the latest wave or wind of doctrine. A basic false teaching of any new "movement" is always that "we must be on the cutting edge." Those on the cutting edge might be cut to ribbons by deceiving spirits. If we abide in Christ, God is not so unrighteous as to make us "miss the boat" or be left out of what He is doing in these last days. This spirit of fear of missing out is designed to get us to accept Charismatic nonsense.

Furthermore, the apostles themselves did not think that they were in the flesh, causing division, or sowing discord when they identified people they were correcting. Jude says sometimes we have to contend for the faith (verse 3). The disciple of love rebukes Diotrephes by name in III John 9. The apostle Paul immediately before warning about getting in the flesh, says, "You were running well; who hindered you from obeying the truth? This persuasion did not come from Him who calls you. A little leaven leavens the whole lump. Would that those who are troubling you would even mutilate themselves" (Galatians 5:7-9,12).

I also received a prophecy from Dick Mills. He said that I was to "cry at the head of every street," and that the following three verses applied to me in this present situation:

1. "But you, be strong and do not lose courage, for there is reward for your work" (II Chronicles 15:7).

2. "Does not wisdom call, and understanding lift up her voice? On top of the heights beside the way, where

the paths meet, she takes her stand; beside the gates, at the opening to the city, at the entrance of the doors, she cries out" (Proverbs 8:13).

3. "And let us not lose heart in doing good, for in due time we shall reap if we do not grow weary" (Galatians 6:9).

You must also know I have heard from 45 pastors in the Kansas City area. One pastor's letter could be considered neutral. The other 44 pastors solidly supported my position with KCF. They said things like this:

"Someone had to preach this message."

"You were the only one who had the credibility in the city to do it."

"No one can accuse you of being insecure or jealous because your church is a lot larger than Kansas City Fellowship."

"I'm an Assembly of God pastor and so I could not have preached the message. I'm sorry you had to do it but it needed to be done."

Interview

A YEAR BEFORE HE DIED, Pastor Ernie Gruen was interviewed by a blogger. This was 18 years after he had preached the sermon "Do We Keep Smiling and Say Nothing?" and produced his follow-up document, "Aberrant Practices," an investigation into Mike Bickle's church.

"Did you ever hear the rumor that you recanted 'Aberrant Practices?' If so, what was your reaction?"

"I was more disappointed than shocked. I was disappointed that Mike Bickle and/or his IHOP staff would deliberately spread lies. I receive several emails a month asking me if I recanted."

"What were you going through when you wrote your report?"

"I really received tremendous support locally, and was not attacked by other ministers, so I was at peace."

"We know that Kansas City Fellowship taught about a 'new breed,' i.e., 'The Omega Generation.' Would you mind expounding on it a bit? Also, do you think they have ceased teaching on this doctrine?"

"They will not quit teaching any doctrine that makes them elitist."

"Did you truly exonerate Paul Cain from all your previous accusations? If so, would you mind telling us what changed your mind?"

"Mike Bickle himself exposed and discredited him."

"Did you really apologize to Mr. Bickle for the accusations you made in your report?"

"This fabrication that I apologized, spread by Mike Bickle and/or his IHOP staff, is a total lie. I never apologized to him—you do not apologize for exposing false prophets and telling the truth."

"Do you think that John Wimber's covering addressed the problems you spoke of in your report?"

"The elders of Full Faith Church agreed to stop sending out the 'Aberrant Document' for two reasons: firstly, John Wimber said he would 'clean up the mess at KCF' and provide oversight; and, secondly, to restore unity in the city. However, before Wimber died, he phoned me and said I was right all the time in the 'Aberrant Document,' and that he regretted getting involved with Mike Bickle. The proof that this phone call occurred is that at this point KCF quit calling themselves 'Metro Vineyard,' and removed themselves from his covering."

"Do you think that the International House Of Prayer (**IHOP**) is spiritually dangerous? If so, what concerns you the most?"

"Please read an excerpt from an email I received this week:

> Last year I attended the "Fire in the Night" internship at the **IHOP**. It had a class called "Prophetic History." We listened to audio tapes of Mike Bickle's experiences in the supernatural realm and prophecies of Bob Jones and Paul Cain. After some meetings with the leadership there I decided to leave the program. I was led to the report you had written about the Kansas City Prophets and Mike Bickle exposing them for their lies. After reading this report I was even more disturbed because of its content. I took what I had read back to the leadership at **IHOP** and presented it to them, asking them if the report you wrote was true. They then told me that it was not true and that you had made a public apology to Mike and others for having written it. The leader I spoke to said he was there to witness these things taking place. I wasn't sure if he was telling the truth so I wanted to ask you a couple of questions personally.

"I challenge Mike Bickle and/or IHOP staff to remove this so-called leader for telling a whopper of a lie! Mike Bickle and/or IHOP staff have built their entire foundation on two discredited false prophets. I Cor. 3:11 says: 'For no other foundation can anyone lay than that which is laid, which is Jesus Christ' (NKJV)."

"If there was any advice you could give to someone who is considering worshipping at IHOP, what would it be?"

"Thoroughly read and study two documents and then pray and make your own decision: 1) the original 'Documentation of the Aberrant Practices and Teachings of Kansas City Fellowship'; and, 2) Paul Cain discredited by Mike Bickle."

"Do you feel that the stand you took was worth it?"

"Absolutely!"

Testimony

MY HUSBAND AND I were a part of Kansas City Fellowship from its inception in the early 1980s. In fact, when Mike Bickle first arrived in Kansas City, he spoke at a women's Bible study I was attending. I was so intrigued by his new teaching, I made it a point to attend his soon-to-be new church.

From its early days we were led to believe Kansas City Fellowship was commissioned by God with a very special purpose. We were encouraged to read about the modern revivals, such as Azusa Street; as well as the modern revivalists, such as Maria Woodworth-Etter and Charles Finney. We were also encouraged to read about the life of David Brainerd, especially his devotion to prayer. Also on the list of required reading were all of Kenneth Hagin's books. All of this was to prepare us for the coming revival.

KCF was set up by a false prophet. Augustine Alcala, the original "prophet" who spoke to Mike back in St. Louis, prophesied that Mike needed to move to Kansas City to begin this new move of God. He was later dismissed as false when a certain prophecy never came to pass. He was also later discovered to have a hidden homosexual lifestyle that was exposed before he passed away. But he needs to be included in the Kansas City Prophets head count, because he was highly esteemed and credited from the beginning as a true prophet.

Mike's main focus in the early days was to pray for God to pour out His Holy Spirit as He did in the days of Acts. During the first year when Bob Jones came on the scene, this focus remained the same with the added oohing and awwing associated with having our own resident prophet. We were so flattered regarding our calling to be *the* elite group that would usher in *the revival to beat all revivals.*

Jones told us we had been invited to pray this thing in. He had all kinds of remarkable tales of God having promised him through the years that a generation would arise in his future that would someday receive him. *We* were that special generation.

During the first year of the new church, both Mike Bickle and Bob Jones received a personal visitation from the angel Gabriel. He gave both of them the same Scriptures, the Book of Daniel Chapter 9, and told both to call a solemn assembly.

Our leaders obeyed the angel and called a solemn assembly. We were called to fast and pray for 21 days. At the end of it the Lord was going to fill us with His Holy Spirit as He did on the Day of Pentecost.

We all began the long fast with great anticipation. We then spent many days and nights binding and loosing territorial spirits, a trendy new spiritual technique, in order to open up the heavenlies so God could pour His Spirit down. At the end of the long fast, however, *absolutely nothing happened.*

What happened? Why was there no revival? It was "discovered" by our leaders that we didn't have the proper "wineskin" in place to receive the new wine promised by the angel Gabriel.

So, while continuing our routine to pray every night and day for the Lord to send His Spirit, they started "Commitment Classes." These lasted for about two years. Absolutely anyone who wanted to participate in any kind of ministry at the church, be it on the worship team, or volunteering with the children, had to attend these classes. The gist of the teaching was church government and how the city needed an apostolic leader over all the churches in order for the believers to contain this level of anointing. I kid you not.

These were the most boring classes to attend, but attend them we did, because noone wanted to miss the prophesied special "move of God," and everyone wanted a leadership-type position.

It was during this time that the prophets were on the move, prophesying to churches to submit to Mike, or else they would be left out. It was also at this time that my husband and I both began to become seriously confused.

Our lives had become too busy to continue attending the nightly prayer meetings. We were a young growing family with toddlers to raise. The prophecies were confusing and very "cosmic" in nature. The ones that were clear enough to follow were not coming to pass.

More importantly, those of us attending the nightly prayer meetings noticed the original "vision" changed. We had been on board for the "pray night and day until" vision, but the rules kept changing, and Mike was becoming a sensation.

Many ministries throughout the United States and even England were embracing his "city church" vision, and were equally wowed by the prophets. When the Vineyard began showing interest, they appeared more influenced by Mike and the prophets than the other way around.

One important fact never gets mentioned and has since been removed from the history. Mike had a paraplegic brother named Pat who always attended the evening prayer meetings. The early prayer movement only had about a dozen regulars, so we got to know one another quite well.

Amongst all the prophecies and promises of the Spirit being poured out on us, there was *always* the promise that Pat would be healed. So often was that promise repeated that we spoke of it as a "given." All of the prophets mentioned it numerous times. In fact, it was going to be the event that started the whole ball rolling, the sign of imminent revival.

Sadly, Pat passed away a few years ago. His often-stated prophecy, at least how pivotal it was, got erased from the history. Now when new IHOPers listen to the 18-plus hours of how IHOP came to be, their "Prophetic History," they won't know about Pat and the profound promise that we hoped for in his healing.

It was at this time that my husband and I set aside all the nonsense we had been taught—all the false teachings and false prophecies—and turned to the Scriptures alone for guidance. The Lord graciously revealed the gospel to us and our confusion ceased.

The Message of the Cross was not being preached at Kansas City Fellowship. My husband tried to talk to Mike about it several times, but was not received well. When Ernie Gruen preached his memorable sermon "Do We Keep Smiling and Say Nothing?" we left. His message helped us see the error of the whole prophetic thing.

Back then I assumed this whole thing would just fizzle out. How wrong I was! We now have grown children who rub elbows with other grown children influenced by IHOP. Although our children have been taught the error of this movement, I find it necessary to reteach *why* it is wrong, especially since so many churches here in Kansas City have people in their congregations who also attend IHOP.

Index

60 percent 11
1980s 41
Absorption 21
Acts 18 29
Agape Ministries 7
Aggressive Prophetic
  Expansion 18, 21
Alexander 6
angel 8
angels 2, 8, 9, 10, 12, 13
anointing 43
apostles 6, 14, 34
Assembly of God 19, 20,
  22, 35
Augustine Alcala 42
baby 9
Bill Newby 19, 20
Bob Jones 42
Charisma magazine 11
Charismatic Pastors
  Fellowship 13, 14, 19,
  27

children 12, 13, 17, 33
Christ 1, 2, 3, 7, 8, 25,
  28, 29, 34, 40
church government 43
Colossians 2, 6, 23
Commitment Classes 43
Cursed 23
dead 11
death 17, 29
deceitful 25, 33
defraud 7, 8
demons 13
dream 5, 26
elders 11, 13, 15, 17, 18,
  21, 22, 38
Exaltation of Man 21
fabrication 11, 14, 38
false prophets 1, 2, 3, 4,
  5, 38, 40
false teaching 14, 34
fast 43
Gabriel 42, 43

Government by Prophets 15, 16
Grandview 21
heresy 14, 15, 29, 33
homosexual 15, 42
hurt 7
Hymenaeus 6
IHOP 37, 38, 39, 40, 45, 46
integrity 20, 23, 27, 32
Jambres 6
Jannes 6
Jeffrey Lundgren 3
Jesus 1, 4, 5, 6, 12, 21, 25, 28, 40
Kansas City Fellowship 9, 16, 21, 22, 27, 28, 30, 31, 35, 38, 40, 41, 45
Kansas City Prophets 42
KCF 13, 17, 18, 20, 22, 26, 31, 32, 33, 35, 38
Larry Lea 16
Maranatha 13
Matthew 18 17, 18, 28
Matthew 24 1, 4, 5
Mike Bickle 13, 19, 27, 28, 29, 37, 38, 39, 40, 42
monasticism 8
Monastic Mysticism 18
money 8, 10, 21, 22
mother 9
pastor 8, 10, 11, 14, 15, 16, 18, 19, 35

Pat 44, 45
Pied Piper 23
prayer meetings 44
prophecies 4, 9, 10, 11, 12, 16, 20, 22, 27, 28, 30, 39, 44, 45
prophecy 9, 10, 11, 20, 21, 23, 24, 25, 26, 31, 34, 45
snow 9
prophesy 11, 18, 20
prophesying 44
prophet 4, 9, 10, 11, 15, 18, 19, 21, 24
Prophetic History 45
prophets 1, 2, 3, 4, 5, 9, 10, 14, 15, 17, 20, 38, 40, 44, 45
Receiving 13, 14
revival 41, 43, 45
Roman Catholicism 14
self-abasement 2, 3, 7, 8, 13, 23
solemn assembly 42
spider 5
Supposed Submission 14
territorial spirits 43
unethical 19, 20, 23, 28
Usurpation 16
vision 20, 21, 33, 44
visions 2, 12, 13
wife 5, 17, 25, 29

About The Author

ERNEST J. GRUEN was a pastor and author. From 1961 to 1966 he was pastor of Wyandotte Baptist Church in Kansas City. Then he became the founder of, and was senior pastor at, Full Faith Church of Love in Shawnee, Kansas. Full Faith began with seven families meeting in a basement in June 1966. In 1980 it moved to 6824 Lackman Road, about 45 minutes from Downtown Kansas City. Over 27 years he built Full Faith into an independent church that was charismatic and non-denominational. By the 1990s FFCL had become a megachurch with 3,500 attending weekly services. It had four network churches; 10,000 attended weekly. It sponsored Maranatha Academy, a nearby K-12 Christian school with 600 students. Gruen was on radio for 25 years and on TV for 10. His Sunday church services were broadcast locally. He and his wife Delores (Dee) had four children. He died on June 1, 2009; he was 72.

Books by Ernie Gruen

Freedom to Choose (1976)

Freedom to Grow (1983)

Touching the Heart of God (1986)

The Giver and His Gifts (2000)

But God Gives More Grace (2003)

Cleansing Your Heart of Anger and Bitterness (2005)

Made in the USA
Las Vegas, NV
15 January 2024

84386935R10038